what would you ask?
AMELIA EARHART

Anita Ganeri
Illustrated by Liz Roberts

Belitha Press

First published in the UK in 1999 by
Belitha Press Limited, London House,
Great Eastern Wharf, Parkgate Road,
London SW11 4NQ

ISBN 1 85561 896 6

British Library Cataloguing in Publication Data for
this book is available from the British Library.

Printed in China

Editor: Veronica Ross
Designer: Simeen Karim
Illustrator: Liz Roberts
Consultant: Hester Collicutt

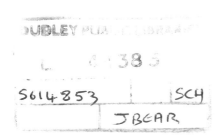

Contents

What do you do?

'I'm an American pilot and explorer.'

In 1928, American pilot Amelia Earhart became the first woman
to fly across the Atlantic Ocean. She made many more
record-breaking flights and became one of the
most famous women in the world.

At that time, flying was still very dangerous. But Amelia used her fame to show that women were equal with men, and she became a role model for millions of women. In 1937, Amelia set off on a daring adventure to fly around the world at the equator. No one had tried this route before. Two-thirds of the way through the journey, her plane disappeared in the Pacific Ocean. Amelia Earhart was never seen again.

NR·965·Y

Where were you born?

'I was born in Atchison, Kansas, USA.'

Amelia was born on 24 July 1897 in her grandparents' house in the small town of Atchison, Kansas. She had one sister, Muriel, who was three years younger.

Soon after Amelia was born, her family moved to Kansas City and then to Des Moines in Iowa, where Amelia's father worked as a lawyer. Amelia adored her father, who was kind and loving. But he was also fond of drinking with his friends. In the end, this lost him his job.

Once more the Earharts moved, this time to St Paul, Minnesota. Money was tight and the family had to watch every penny they spent. When Mr Earhart decided to return to Kansas City, Amelia and Muriel moved with their mother to Chicago.

What were you like as a child?

'A bit of a tomboy. I liked doing things my own way.'

Amelia worked hard at school and especially liked science, literature and French. But she did not mix much with the other girls. She and Muriel spent their holidays at their grandparents' house. There were plenty of places to explore, and Amelia's daredevil nature often landed her in trouble. She liked to jump over fences instead of using the gate. She even hunted rats with a rifle.

One summer, when Amelia was seven years old, her father took her to a fair. Amelia thought that the roller coaster was the most thrilling thing she had ever seen. When she got home, she built her own in the back yard. The first run ended in a crash landing but Amelia didn't mind.
It was just like flying.

Did you always want to be a pilot?

'Not really. But after I visited an airfield,
I knew I had to fly.'

Amelia left high school in 1916, aged 18. In 1917, she spent
Christmas with her sister in Toronto, Canada. The First World
War was raging in Europe, and Canada was playing its part. The
hospitals were full of wounded soldiers. Amelia at once decided
to become a Red Cross nurse. For almost a year she scrubbed
floors, cooked meals and
gave out medicines in
a military hospital.

Despite the long hours, Amelia still had fun. Some Canadian pilots invited her to watch a display of stunt-flying. Suddenly, one of the pilots dived straight at the crowd. Instead of running away in fear, Amelia was thrilled. She knew she too had to fly.

Before long, flying had become the most important thing in Amelia's life. To earn money to pay for flying lessons, Amelia worked as a telephone clerk, photographer, truck driver, teacher and social worker.

How did you learn to fly?

'I asked my father to let me have some flying lessons. He wasn't very keen at first!'

In December 1920, Amelia's father took her to an air show in California where there was a daring display of racing, aerobatics and wing-walking. The next day, he paid for her first ever flight. Amelia never looked back. Early in 1921, when she was 23, Amelia had her first flying lesson. Her teacher was Neta Snook, one of the very few women pilots. Amelia learned quickly.

Within a few weeks, she took the plane up into the air. Later that year, she made her first solo flight.

Amelia saved hard, and a year later, on her 25th birthday, she became the proud owner of her own aeroplane. She found out all she could about her new plane and how the engine worked. Amelia painted the plane yellow and nicknamed it *The Canary*.

Later that year she had her first crash and landed in a cabbage patch. The accident put her off cabbages, she told her friends, but not flying.

Where was your first long flight?

'In 1928 I flew across the Atlantic Ocean.'

In 1927, American pilot Charles Lindbergh had made the first solo flight across the Atlantic in his aeroplane, *Spirit of St Louis*. The following year Amelia received a phone call from Captain Hilton H Riley, who had been a wartime pilot. He asked Amelia if she would become the first woman to fly the Atlantic Ocean.

Amelia accepted eagerly. One morning in June 1928, she joined the seaplane *Friendship* ready for take-off from Newfoundland in Canada. Amelia's job was to note down details of their speed, height and direction.

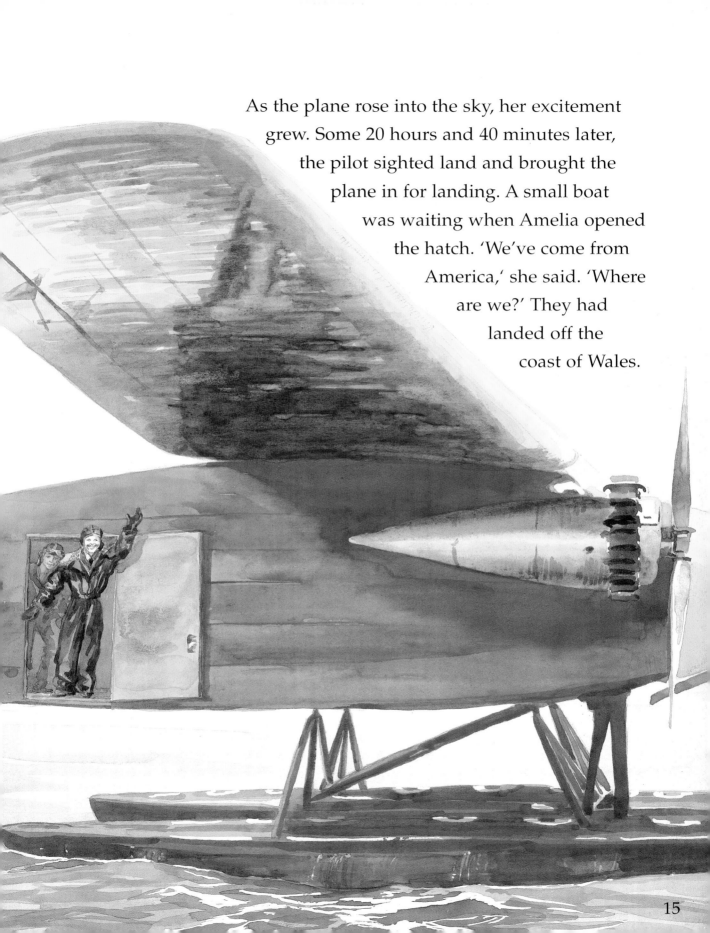

As the plane rose into the sky, her excitement grew. Some 20 hours and 40 minutes later, the pilot sighted land and brought the plane in for landing. A small boat was waiting when Amelia opened the hatch. 'We've come from America,' she said. 'Where are we?' They had landed off the coast of Wales.

What was life like after that flight?

'It was very different in many ways.'

Amelia returned home from her Atlantic flight to find she had become famous. Wherever she went, huge crowds of people flocked to see her. Amelia's name was splashed across all the newspapers. She was known as the First Lady of the Air.

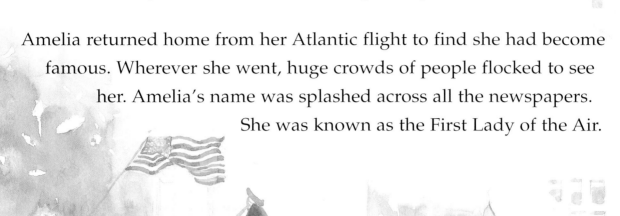

Amelia wrote a book about her flight, called *20 Hours, 40 Minutes*, the time the journey had taken. She gave hundreds of speeches, lectures and interviews. She used her fame to encourage people to travel on the first passenger aircraft. She often went on the flights herself, chatting to passengers and signing autographs. In 1929, Amelia helped to set up the Ninety-Nines, a club for women pilots.

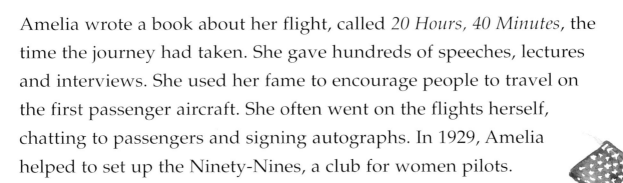

In 1931, Amelia married George Putnam, a wealthy businessman. He had organized the Atlantic flight and now he wanted to make her the most famous woman in America.

What were your other greatest adventures?

'There were lots more records to set. I wanted to show people how good women pilots could be.'

Despite her fame, Amelia was not contented. She still wanted to prove herself as a pilot. In 1930, Amelia flew faster than any woman before. And in 1932, she set out on her greatest adventure yet – to fly solo across the Atlantic.

The journey would be difficult – some said impossible. But Amelia took off from Newfoundland and, despite many dangers, landed safely in a field in Ireland. She was the first woman to fly alone across the Atlantic, and had set a new record of 13 hours and 30 minutes for the journey. She was also the first person to make the crossing twice.

Back home, Amelia was showered with awards. She became friends with kings and presidents, film stars and explorers. But she was always happiest up in the air, away from the crowds.

Were you ever scared?

'Yes, sometimes. But it didn't put me off. I loved flying too much.'

In Amelia's time, pilots had to be very brave. Planes were poorly built and accidents were common. Amelia had her fair share of crashes. Planes could be brought down by bad weather or engine failure, and pilots sometimes lost their way in the dark.

On Amelia's solo flight across the Atlantic, she flew straight into a storm. Ice formed on the plane, which went into a spin. Through the blackness below, she could see the ocean waves. Luckily, as the plane lost height, the warmer air melted the ice. Amelia was able to right the plane and hold it level. Just in time.

In 1935, Amelia made the first solo flight from Hawaii to California, across the Pacific Ocean. For most of the way, she flew in thick fog. A cover blew off part of the cockpit and freezing air poured into the cabin. When Amelia finally landed, she knew she was lucky to be alive.

What sort of aeroplane did you fly?

'For my round-the-world trip, I was given a new plane, called a Lockheed Electra.'

In 1936, Amelia began to think about one more long flight. This would be her last, she said. Then she would take life easy. She wanted to fly around the world at the equator, something no one had tried before. For this trip, she needed a new and more powerful plane.

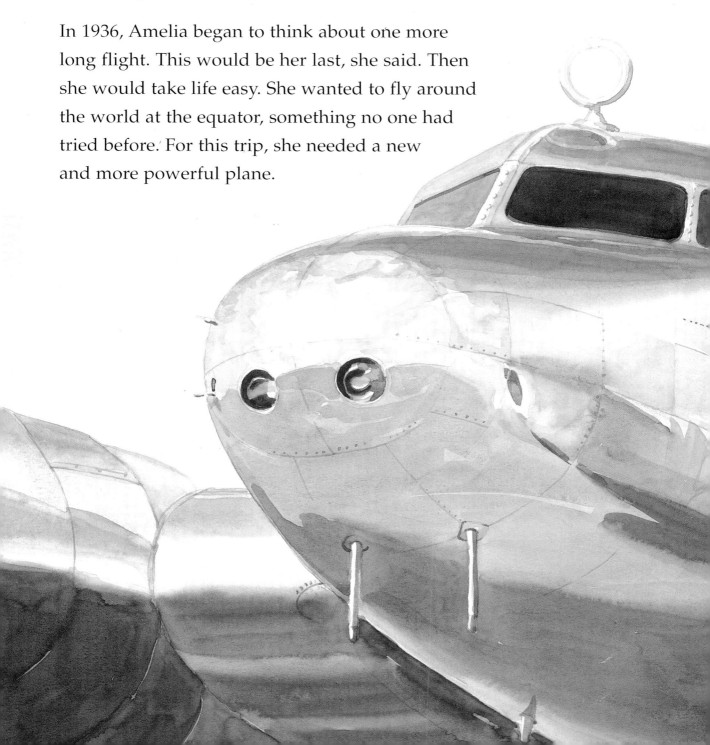

A year earlier, Amelia had taken a post at a university helping women plan careers in engineering and mechanics. The university set up a fund to buy Amelia the plane of her dreams – a Lockheed Model 10E Electra. It was the sleekest, most modern plane Amelia had ever owned.

The Electra had two engines so that it could still fly if one engine failed. It had space for a navigator – this would be too long a journey to fly alone – and so many gadgets that Amelia nicknamed it the *Flying Laboratory*. Amelia practised flying it every day, especially take-offs and landings.

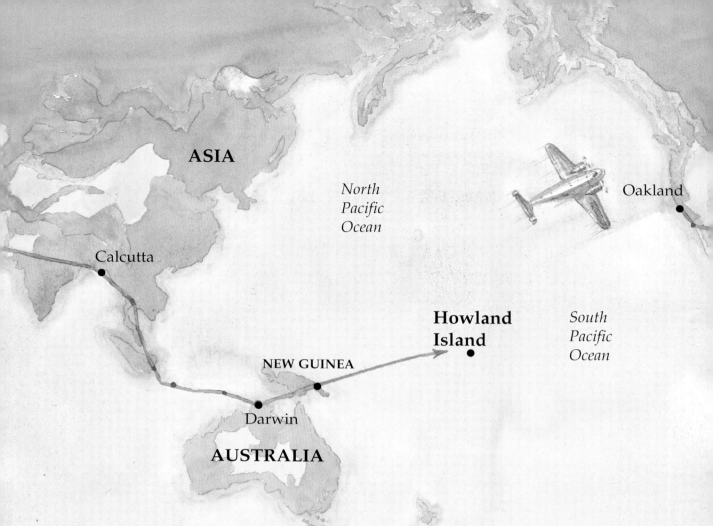

ASIA

North
Pacific
Ocean

Oakland

Calcutta

Howland
Island

South
Pacific
Ocean

NEW GUINEA

Darwin

AUSTRALIA

Amelia's last flight

Amelia's round-the-world flight took a year to plan. After several delays, she and her navigator, a man called Fred Noonan, took off from Oakland, California on 20 May 1937. For a month, they flew eastwards, along the coast of South America, across the Atlantic to Africa and Asia, then to the island of New Guinea. They crossed jungles, seas, deserts and mountains.

But the most dangerous part of the journey was still to come. From New Guinea, Amelia had to fly to Howland Island, a tiny speck of land in the middle of the Pacific Ocean. It was extremely tricky to find. Early on 2 July, Amelia steered the Electra down the runway and into the air.

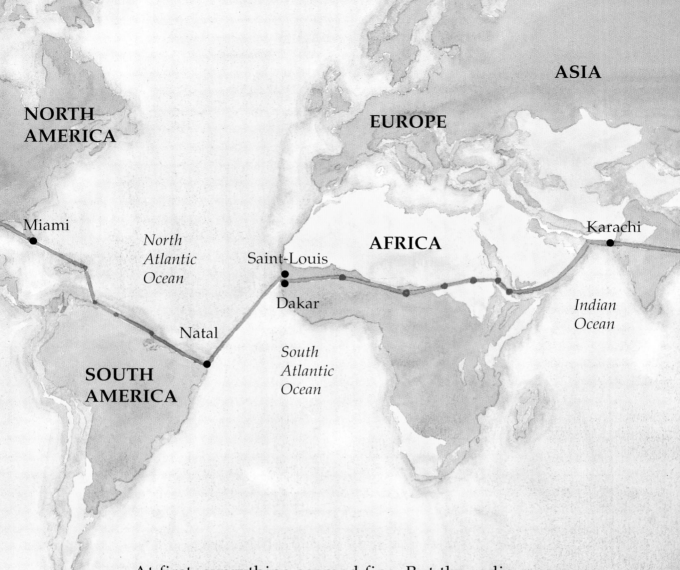

NORTH
AMERICA

EUROPE

ASIA

Miami

*North
Atlantic
Ocean*

Saint-Louis

AFRICA

Karachi

Dakar

*Indian
Ocean*

Natal

SOUTH
AMERICA

*South
Atlantic
Ocean*

At first, everything seemed fine. But the radio messages from Amelia soon grew fainter. The last call came the following morning. Fuel was running low, Amelia said, and they could not see land. Then the radio went dead. The plane never reached the island. Despite a huge search, no trace of Amelia, Noonan or the Electra was ever found.

Amelia Earhart was just 39 years old when she died. But in her short life, she inspired millions of people all over the world. Through her kindness, courage and determination, she showed everyone, especially women, that dreams can come true.

The Lockheed Electra

The Lockheed Electra 10E was the plane flown by Amelia on her last flight around the world.

The 10E Electra had a wingspan of 17 metres, a body length of 11.5 metres and a height of 3 metres.

Only 15 10E Electras were made by the Lockheed company in the USA. The first was made in 1934.

The 10E's maximum speed was 325 kilometres per hour.

The 10E Electra was the first all-metal passenger aircraft. It had two engines, and was the only plane large and powerful enough to carry the fuel needed for the long stages of Amelia's flight.

Empty, the 10E Electra weighed 2927 kilograms. With its crew and heavy fuel load, this increased to 7121 kilograms.

At maximum speed, the 10E Electra could fly from New York to California in about 13.5 hours. Today's newest plane, the Boeing 777 would take just four hours to complete the journey.

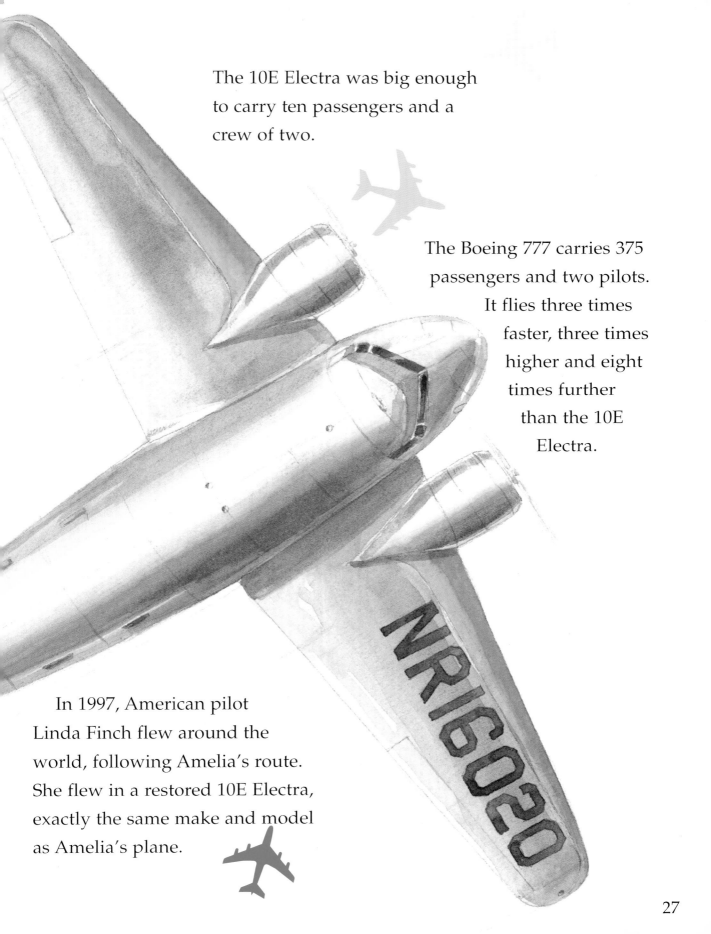

The 10E Electra was big enough to carry ten passengers and a crew of two.

The Boeing 777 carries 375 passengers and two pilots. It flies three times faster, three times higher and eight times further than the 10E Electra.

In 1997, American pilot Linda Finch flew around the world, following Amelia's route. She flew in a restored 10E Electra, exactly the same make and model as Amelia's plane.

Some important dates

1903 The Wright brothers make the first-ever powered flight.

1897 Amelia Earhart is born in Atchison, Kansas, USA, on 24 July.

1916 Amelia finishes high school in Chicago.

1917 Amelia works as a Red Cross nurse in a military hospital in Toronto, Canada.

1919 Amelia becomes a student at Columbia University.

1920 Amelia takes her first flight, as a passenger.

1921 Amelia starts to take flying lessons from Neta Snook, one of the very few women pilots. Later that year, Amelia makes her first solo flight.

1922 Amelia buys her first aeroplane, nicknamed *The Canary*.

1923 Amelia receives her pilot's licence. She was only the sixteenth woman in the world to have one.

1925-8 Amelia works as a teacher, then a social worker in Boston.

1928 Amelia becomes the first woman to fly across the Atlantic Ocean. She is part of a three-person crew aboard the seaplane *Friendship*. Amelia's book *20 Hours, 40 Minutes* is published.

1929 Amelia flies in the first ever Women's Air Derby, in which she finishes third. She also helps to found the Ninety-Nines, an international club for women pilots.

1930 Amelia flies faster than any woman before, at 290 kilometres per hour.

1931 Amelia marries George Putnam, a wealthy publisher and businessman.

1932 Amelia becomes the first woman to fly across the Atlantic Ocean solo. She receives the gold medal from the National Geographic Society, and the Distinguished Flying Cross.

1935 Amelia makes the first solo flight from Hawaii to California. She also becomes the first person to fly non-stop from Mexico City to Newark, New Jersey, USA. She joins Purdue University to advise women on careers in engineeering and mechanics.

1937 Amelia sets out to fly around the world at the equator.

1937 On 3 July, Amelia's plane disappears in the Pacific Ocean, before she reaches Howland Island.

1964 An American pilot, Joan Merriam Smith, finally becomes the first woman to fly around the world, following Amelia's route. This route becomes known as the Earhart Trail.

1997 Linda Finch flies around the world, following Amelia's route, in a restored 10E Electra.

Glossary

aerobatics Flying an aircraft in a daring or spectacular way, for fun or to entertain people.

cockpit The part of an aeroplane where the pilot and crew sit and operate the plane.

daredevil A person who acts without any thought of danger.

equator An imaginary line around the middle of the earth. Amelia's route round the equator was 46,000 kilometres long.

First World War The First World War broke out in 1914 between the Allies (Britain, France, Russia and, in 1917, the USA) and the Central Powers (Germany, Turkey and Austria-Hungary). Countries in the British Empire, including Canada, also fought. The Allies won the war. By the time the war ended in 1918, some 10 million soldiers had been killed in battle.

Charles Lindbergh (1902–1974) An American pilot who made the first non-stop solo flight across the Atlantic in 1927. He flew from New York to Paris in 33 hours and 30 minutes.

military To do with the armed forces (the army, navy or air force).

navigator The person who works out the route that a plane follows on a flight. He or she uses maps and instruments to make sure that the plane keeps to that route.

nickname A funny or affectionate name.

Ninety-Nines (**99s**) The club which Amelia Earhart helped to set up in 1929. Its aim was to encourage women pilots. It was called the 99s because it originally had 99 members. Today it is still active, with 70,000 members all over the world.

passenger aircraft An aeroplane which carries passengers.

pilot's licence The licence given to people who have passed their flying exams. They also have to spend a number of hours in the air, some of them flying solo.

Red Cross An international healthcare organization. It was set up in 1863 by a Swiss man who had seen the terrible suffering that war causes. There are now branches of the society in more than a hundred countries.

restore To restore means to bring back. Restoring an old plane, for example, means to bring it back to flying condition.

role model A role model is someone you admire and look up to because of their personality or achievements.

seaplane An aeroplane designed to take off from and land in water.

solo On your own. Flying solo means that you fly on your own, acting as pilot and navigator.

stunt-flying Performing brave or spectacular acts in the air, such as looping the loop and diving low.

wingspan The distance from the tip of one wing to the tip of the other wing.

wing-walking A brave stunt performed at air shows in which one person stands on the plane's wing as the plane flies.

Wright brothers Two American brothers, Orville (1871–1948) and Wilbur (1867–1912) Wright who made the first powered flight on 17 December 1903.

Index